Contemporary Designs
for Glass Etching

Contemporary Designs for Glass Etching

Sherri Boldt

DOVER PUBLICATIONS, INC.
Mineola, New York

For Rinetto

Bibliographical Note

Contemporary Designs for Glass Etching is a new work, first published by Dover Publications, Inc., in 2005.

DOVER *Pictorial Archive* SERIES

Library of Congress Cataloging-in-Publication Data

Boldt, Sherri.
    Contemporary designs for glass etching / Sherri Boldt.
        p. cm. — (Dover pictorial archive series)
        ISBN-13: 978-0-486-44534-2
        ISBN-10: 0-486-44534-8
        1. Glass etching. I. Title. II. Series.

TT298.B65 2005
748.6'3—dc22

2005051790

Manufactured in the United States by Courier Corporation
44534802   2013
www.doverpublications.com

Introduction

Whether you want to create a grand entrance to your home, or add a decorative accent to a vase, you will discover that glass etching can be a fun and fulfilling hobby. In this book we have selected sixty-three images specifically designed for use in glass etching projects. Choose from a wide variety of patterns including butterflies, fairies, flowers, hearts, and more. There are also frames, corners, and side elements that can be used with the images or without. Use your imagination to design personalized gifts, eye-catching windows, dramatic doorways—the possibilities are endless!

There are a few different techniques used to make etched glass such as applying etching cream or using a sandblaster. In this book we have included complete instructions for the etching cream process only; however, the patterns can be used for any other method.

Please read all instructions before beginning your project, including any information supplied by the manufacturers. Make sure you follow all safety precautions and that you are in a well-ventilated room. Protect your skin and eyes by wearing long sleeves, rubber gloves, and safety goggles.

If you are interested in learning more about this subject, or want to expand your pattern collection, Dover publishes two books that might be helpful to you: *Glass Etching: 46 Full-Size Patterns with Complete Instructions,* by Robert A. Capp and Robert G. Bush, 0-486-24578-0, and *Designs for Glass Etching: 49 Full-Size Motifs,* by Robert G. Bush, 0-486-26000-3.

Instructions

1. Select a design and enlarge or reduce it to the size needed using a copy machine at a local print shop or an office supply store. If you have scanner, you could also size it on your home computer.

2. Prepare the surface of the glass by wiping it with glass cleaner and a lint-free cloth. Mask off all areas that aren't going to be etched with contact paper to protect it.

3. Cut a piece of clear contact paper large enough to cover the surface you will be etching. Apply the contact paper to the front of the glass following the manufacturer's instructions. By slowly smoothing it along with your hands, or a burnishing tool, you can eliminate the possibility of air bubbles being trapped. If you do get an air bubble, carefully pop it with your X-Acto knife and continue smoothing it down.

4. Position and attach the pattern you have chosen to the back of the glass using double-sided tape.

5. Using an X-Acto knife with a sharp blade, carefully cut and peel away the contact paper where you want the etching to be. You can create a striking image on a clear background by removing the contact paper where you see the black portions of the pattern. Or you can remove the contact paper where you see the white areas for a reverse etching (used mainly for a privacy screen). You will see that some of the patterns also have gray shaded areas. When you are finished etching your project you might consider using stained glass paint, or any other medium in these areas to create an interesting effect.

6. Be careful when cutting out the pattern that your lines are smooth and exact. Don't press too hard with the knife or you can damage the glass. This is the most time consuming part of the project, but worth the effort when you see the finished piece.

7. When you have finished cutting and peeling away the contact paper, wipe the surface with glass cleaner and a lint-free cloth to remove any leftover adhesive. Make sure that all the edges are burnished down firmly and that there are no air bubbles in them. Remove the pattern that is attached on the back. Now it's time to start etching!

8. Depending on the size of your surface you may want to work in small portions at a time. For example, if the area you are working on is large, you might want to divide it up into four portions. Read and follow the manufacturer's instructions before applying the etching cream. Cover your work surface with newspaper to protect it.

9. You can apply the etching cream with a paintbrush or a putty knife depending on the size of the project. Make sure that you use a generous amount and that the etching cream goes on smoothly and evenly. If a bubble forms, you can use the edge of your putty knife to pop it.

10. Leave the etching cream on the glass for the time required (follow the manufacturer's instructions), then scrape it off carefully with your putty knife and rinse thoroughly with water.

11. If working on a large project, you can continue on to the next portion repeating steps 7 through 10.

12. When you are done washing all the etching cream from the glass allow your project to dry. Do not remove the contact paper until you have checked your work for spots you might have missed because of hidden bubbles or uneven application of the etching cream. If you need to fix any spots repeat steps 7 through 10.

13. Clean your glass thoroughly with glass cleaner and allow to dry. When you are completely satisfied with the way your project looks, remove all the contact paper and give it a final cleaning.

Fairy 1

Fairy 2

Fairy 3

Fairy 4

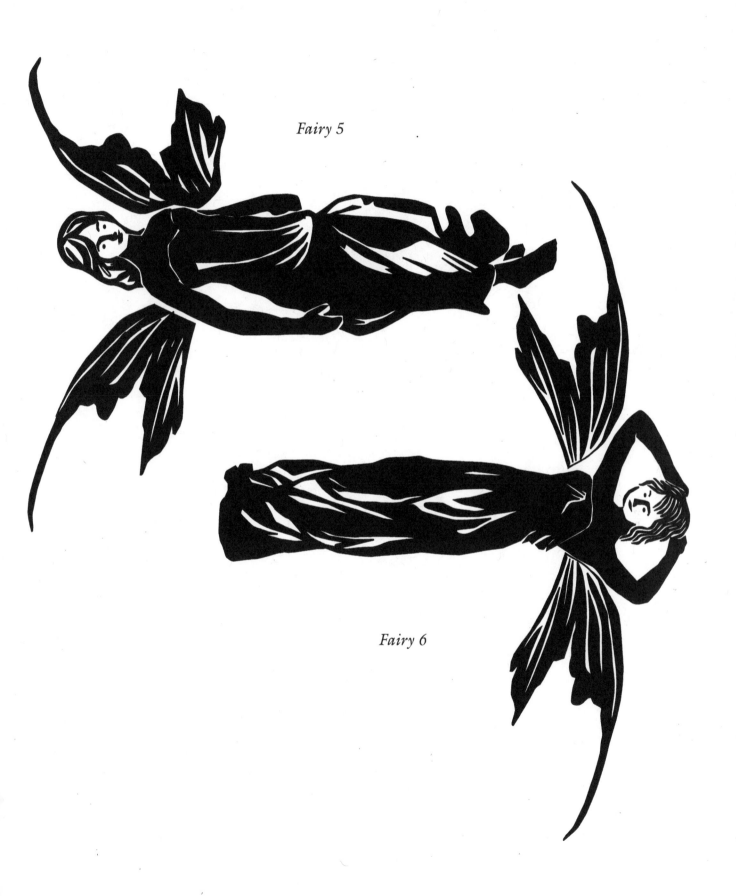

Fairy 5

Fairy 6

Art Nouveau 1

Art Nouveau 2

Art Nouveau 3

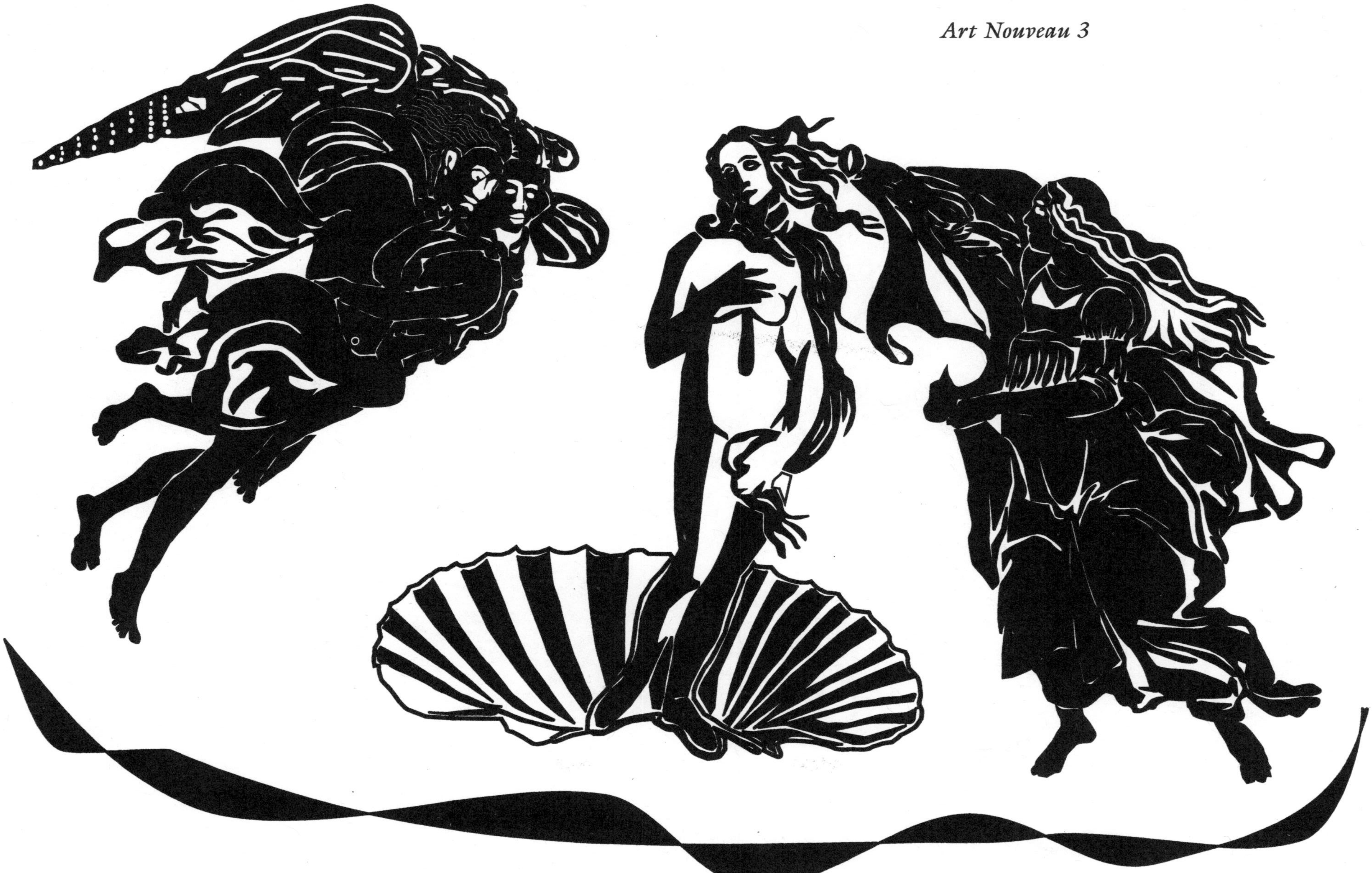

Art Nouveau 4

Dancers in Blue—Edgar Degas

Swans

Owl

Dolphin 1

Dolphin 2

13

Pegasus 1

Butterfly 1

Butterfly 2

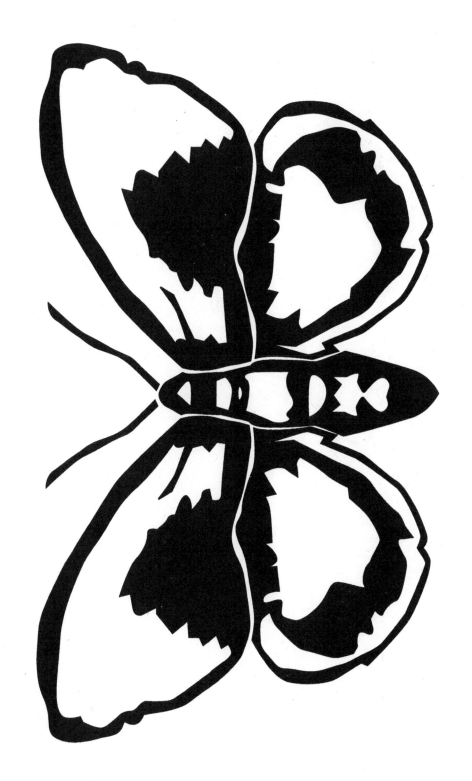

Butterfly 4

Heart 1 (flaming)

Heart 2

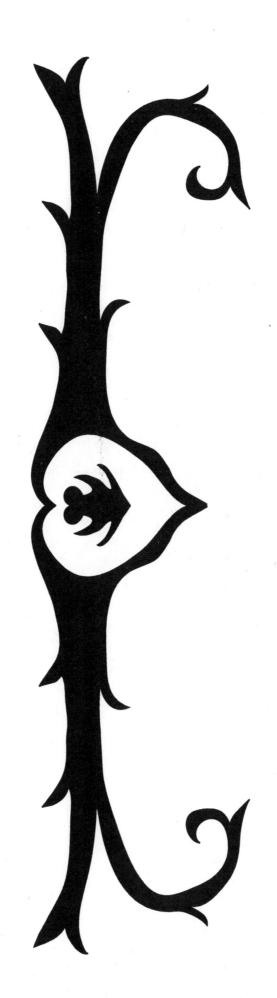

Heart 3

Rose 1

Rose 2

Rose 3

Tribute Roses

Palms in the Wind

Bamboo

Regiment

Tulip Wheel

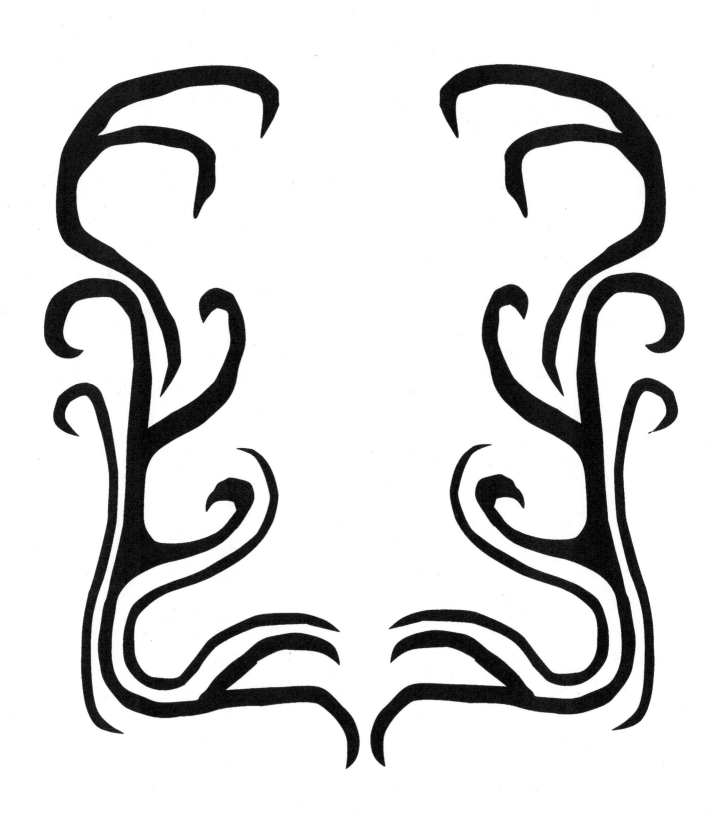

34

Trio

Stars

Candles

Northern Star

Seclusion

Running

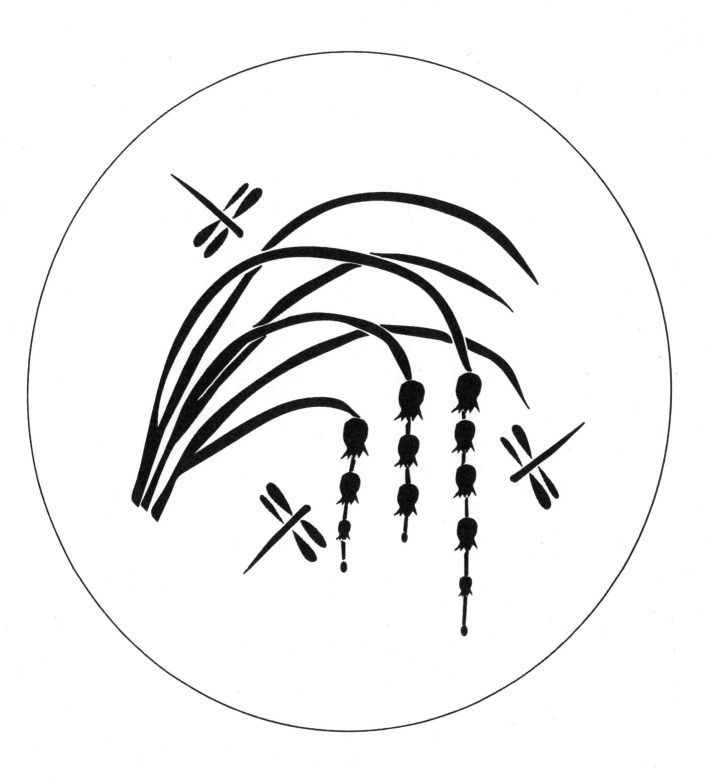

Spring

Cooperation

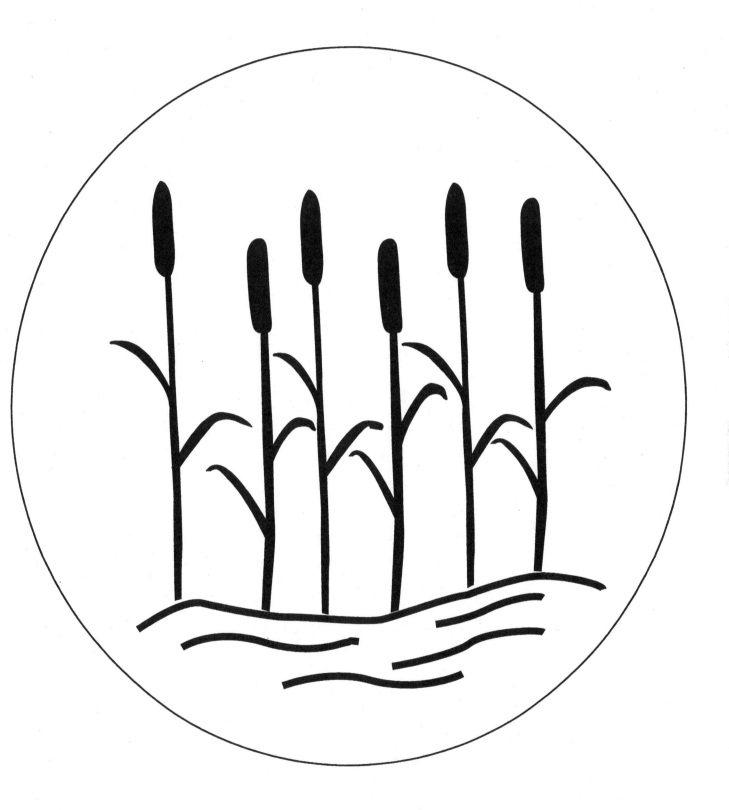

Cattail Cavalry

Beginnings

A Cold Shore

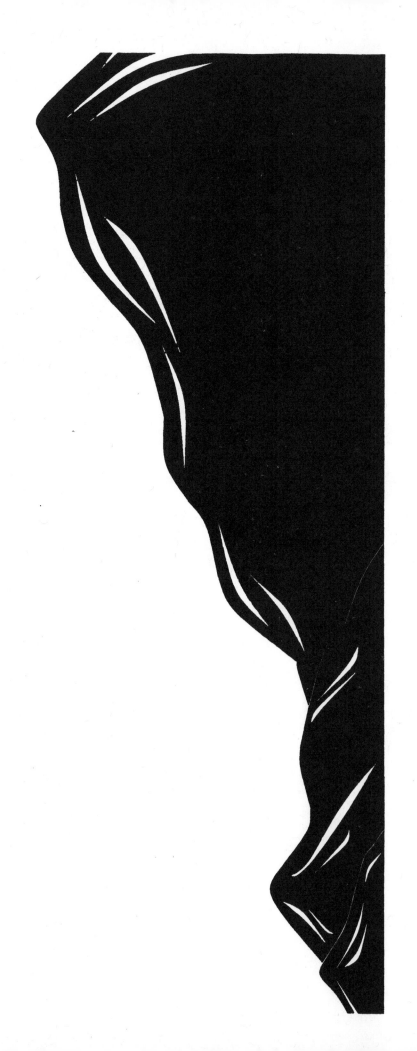

Door Panels 1

Door Panels 2

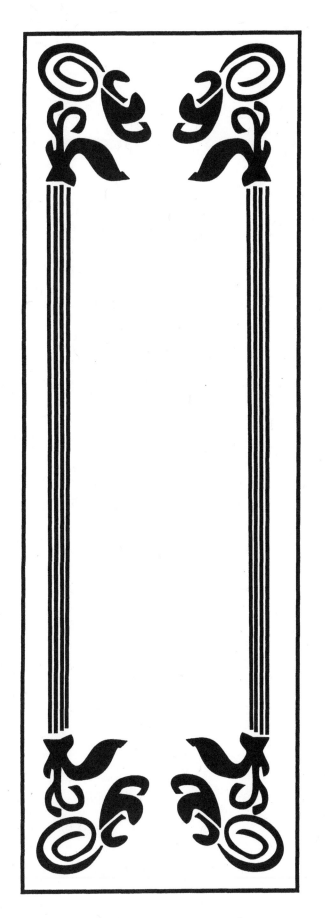
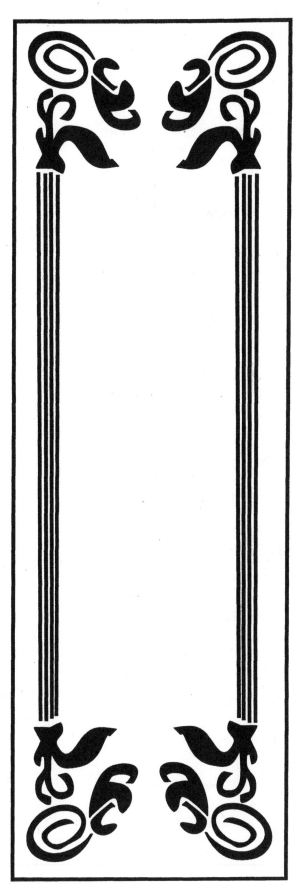

Door Panels 3

50

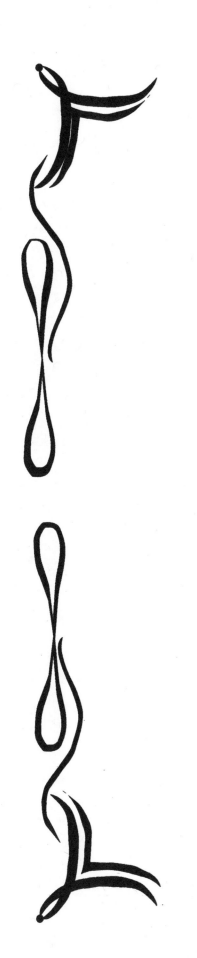

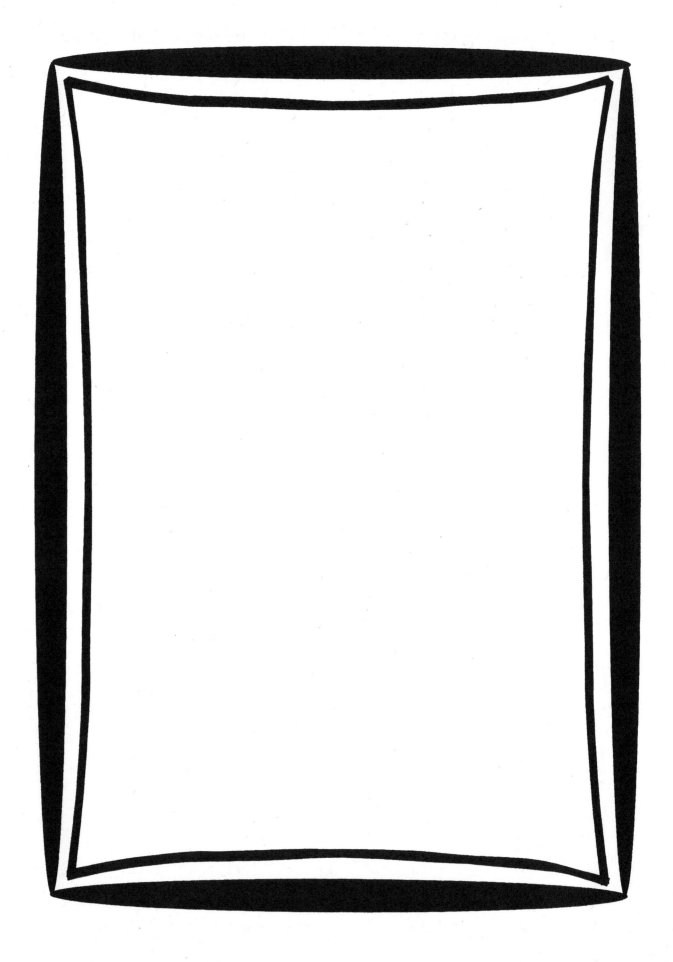

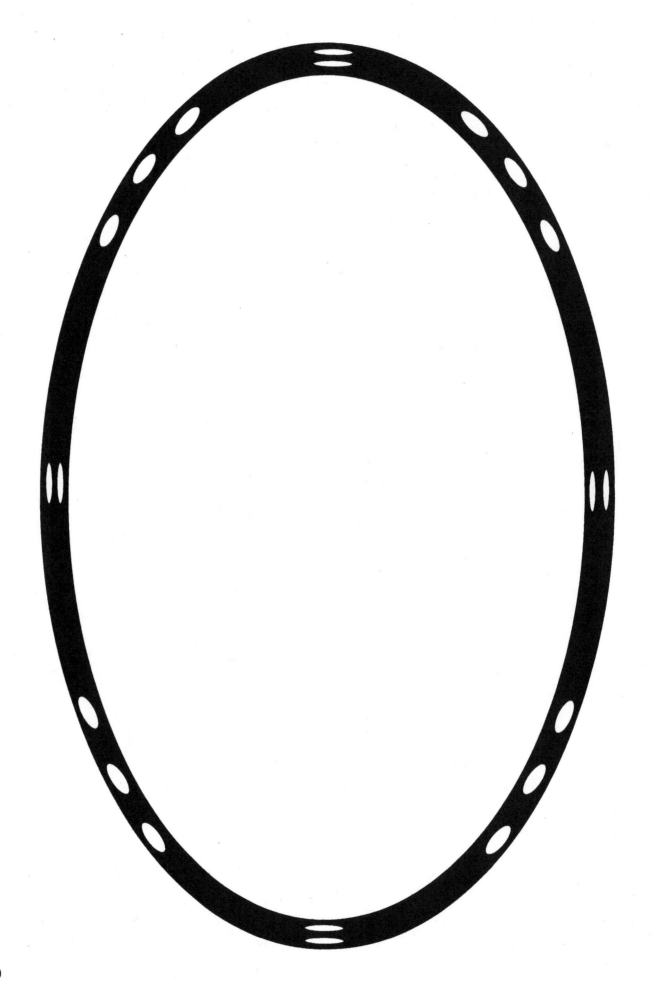